THE CLOUD THAT LIFTED

THE CLOUD THAT LIFTED

BY
MAURICE MAETERLINCK

TRANSLATED BY
F. M. ATKINSON

Fredonia Books
Amsterdam, The Netherlands

The Cloud that Lifted

by
Maurice Maeterlinck

ISBN: 1-4101-0016-2

Copyright © 2002 by Fredonia Books

Reprinted from the 1923 edition

Fredonia Books
Amsterdam, The Netherlands
http://www.fredoniabooks.com

All rights reserved, including the right to reproduce this book, or portions thereof, in any form.

In order to make original editions of historical works available to scholars at an economical price, this facsimile of the original edition of 1923 is reproduced from the best available copy and has been digitally enhanced to improve legibility, but the text remains unaltered to retain historical authenticity.

THE CLOUD THAT LIFTED

DRAMATIS PERSONÆ

AXEL THORILD
TORMASSOV
SONIA BIELENSKY
TATIANA
A SERVANT

The time is the present day, in Finland near Helsingfors.

ACT I

A reception-room in SONIA BIELENSKY'S *house. At the back there are two French-windows opening on the garden, on the left a door leading into the antechamber, on the right a door leading into another drawing-room. The time is evening, with a moon lighting up the garden.*

ACT I

Scene I

[Tormassov; Tatiana.]

Tormassov

For the last four days I have brought together every hint, every little piece of information, listened to every rumour, questioned everybody that might have had the least connection with what has happened, near or remote. The results are not decisive so far, but . . . patience! It is n't humanly possibly that a crime of this kind should vanish into thin air and fade away without leaving some traces. . . . I have unravelled darker puzzles, and I never set about any of

The Cloud That Lifted

them with as much keenness as this one. . . . It would be extraordinary if I couldn't manage what I've done for unknown victims—and sometimes they weren't even of any particular interest— now that it's a question of my very oldest friend. . . . For Bielensky and I, as he must often have told you himself, were boys together; we were linked one to the other, and in a way one through the other, to a fuller and more active past, the very memory of which is fading in these days of overmuch indulgence. We see plainly to-day the abysses to which toleration is dragging us. . . . And the worst is still to come. . . . But let us talk of something else. . . . Where is our poor Sonia? . . . Wretched as her unfortunate father's death is for me, my loss is nothing compared with hers. . . . How is she? . . . Is she a little

The Cloud That Lifted

calmer? . . . What does the doctor say? . . .

TATIANA

She is in her own room. . . . Last night she was a little delirious, but she is asleep now. . . . Since the funeral there has been a kind of relief and reaction. But you know how strong and how brave she is. . . . One single idea rises above her distress and casts a ray of light through it; she is determined to find the assassin and make him pay the penalty.

TORMASSOV

That depends entirely on you; our whole hope rests on you alone. . . .

TATIANA

Alas! I know nothing beyond what I have told you already.

The Cloud That Lifted

Tormassov

And that is of the greatest importance to begin with. You are still convinced that it was an assassination, an ambush? . . .

Tatiana

I have never had the slightest doubt about it.

Tormassov

Still . . . your first impressions, your earliest statements were not so definite.

Tatiana

I was so overwhelmed! . . . I, who had never seen death, that I should see it there all at once, at my feet, in such a guise! . . . In those first moments you are fumbling, puzzling things over, you do not know what you are saying. . . .

The Cloud That Lifted

TORMASSOV

I know, my poor girl. . . . That is why I did not insist. But now that five days have gone by since these first violent emotions, I would be glad to have a more precise statement, to fix once for all just what you do know. . . . I beg you to forgive me for awakening such memories, but it is really absolutely essential. . . . This is a sacrifice I can well claim from your twofold affection for Sonia and for her father who is gone from us. . . . You are our main witness, indeed our only witness, and this is the first time we have been able to talk of these things with the coolness they demand. . . . Try to recall every single one of the details. . . . It often happens that what appears to be least important suddenly becomes the most valuable of all.

The Cloud That Lifted

TATIANA

I don't see that there is very much to add to what I've told you already. . . . As you know, it was on Friday evening. . . . Sonia was away. . . . After dinner I had gone down with her father into the garden. . . . We were strolling in the little alley that goes through the thicket of aspens . . . it was very dark in it. . . . All at once we heard a sound of steps, a rustle of branches brushed aside, and it seems to me—for I am not certain and it might have been nothing more than the cry of an awakened bird—a whistle. . . . Sonia's father quivered—I must tell you that the night before, and that very morning, he had received letters filled with precise and detailed threats—he pulled out the big revolver he always carried after the two attempts on his life

The Cloud That Lifted

last month, and whispered to me, "Don't move; this time I've got the fellow"— and disappeared into the shadows. . . . A few seconds after, I heard a shot, then two more, and finally three successive reports, followed by a cry of distress. . . . I run towards the cry, and nearer than I imagined, in a gleam from the moon, clear of clouds a moment, I see Sonia's father stretched on the ground and just before him, against a wall, the man who had fired, still with his revolver smoking in his hand.

Tormassov
And then?

Tatiana
Then the moon was covered over again, and it grew completely black under the trees; I could distinguish nothing more,

The Cloud That Lifted

and the man disappeared. . . . I don't know how—

TORMASSOV

What sort of man was it?

TATIANA

It's very hard to describe. . . .

TORMASSOV

You had never seen him before?

TATIANA

Never.

TORMASSOV

A young man.

TATIANA

Yes.

The Cloud That Lifted

TORMASSOV

Of what social standing? Rich or poor? A workman, a peasant? . . .

TATIANA

No, of the leisured class.

TORMASSOV

Fair, brown, a beard, no beard? What—

TATIANA

Ah, when it comes to a definite description it becomes very difficult. . . . I am certain that I could easily recognize him in a crowd; and still I feel I could never manage to describe him. . . .

TORMASSOV

Well, let us leave that for the moment. . . . Who do you think fired the first shot?

The Cloud That Lifted

TATIANA

The murderer.

TORMASSOV

What makes you think so? . . .

TATIANA

I'm quite certain of it. . . .

TORMASSOV

We have to make absolutely certain of this point; it is of the utmost importance. . . . Let us see. . . . Can you remember if the sound, the strength, the volume of the six shots were exactly alike?

TATIANA

Yes. . . . Perhaps. . . . Very nearly.

TORMASSOV

I know that such barbarous things are not what girls dream of and ponder,

The Cloud That Lifted

But I will help you. . . . Let's see . . . the revolver Bielensky used, which has been handed over to me, is a service revolver, a heavy-calibre Nagant, of a model that is seldom found in ordinary trade. . . . It is probable, therefore, or nearly certain, that the report it makes must be louder and more violent than that of the murderer's weapon, and so? . . .

TATIANA

Indeed, now I remember. . . . The first shot was a light one, then three more violent, then three not so loud. . . .

TORMASSOV

Just what I expected. . . . The first shot is fired by the murderer. . . . Bielensky replies with the three more violent reports; and that corresponds with the

The Cloud That Lifted

three empty shells found in the chamber of his pistol. . . . That is what we had to prove. The fact is incontestable, and proves beyond dispute that there was an ambush and a premeditated attack. We have a murderer to deal with. . . . And then, to come back to facts, you found the victim lying on the ground? . . .

TATIANA

Yes, across the alley, and not far from the outside wall of the garden. . . . I stooped over him . . . he was in the death-rattle. . . . I raised his head and held it as well as I could. . . . I called out for help, and at last somebody ran up to us. . . .

TORMASSOV

He never spoke?

The Cloud That Lifted

TATIANA

He never said another word.... They carried him to his bed, and he was hardly laid on it before he died without regaining consciousness.... The bullet, as you know, had gone through the nape of the neck and touched the spinal cord....

TORMASSOV

The whistle you mentioned just now, was that a signal?... Do you think the murderer was not alone?...

TATIANA

I had a very clear impression of the flight of several men running in different directions....

TORMASSOV

Were the garden gates shut?

The Cloud That Lifted

TATIANA

The walls are easy to climb. . . .

TORMASSOV

To what extent was he alarmed by the threatening letters he was continually receiving? . . . He never spoke to me about them. . . .

TATIANA

Since the two attempts on his life last month he was always on his guard, suspicious, distrustful, nervous, anxious, but he never spoke of his fears. . . . All the same, I remember once, two days before the murder, while we were talking quietly at night in the drawing-room, he got up quickly and went to the window, exclaiming, "There's somebody prowling about the house." He wanted to go out, to hunt about. . . . We kept him back,

The Cloud That Lifted

thinking it was just nerves that alarmed him, or made him angry, rather, for it roused more anger in him than fear.

TORMASSOV

That was the unlucky thing about it! . . . When anything vexed or thwarted him he would always hurl himself at it like a wild bull. But all this supposes a long expected, coolly planned attempt against him. . . . I had warned him. . . . He had rather a heavy hand lately, and would n't believe in the reawakening of the Scandinavian movement, terrorist or nihilist movement if you like; the name does n't matter a bit, for the three things are one and the same, and it is simply the forces from underneath that are rising up against order. . . . And then in spite of all my advice he went obstinately on living in this old isolated, lonely, dangerous

The Cloud That Lifted

house. But since a crime has actually been committed I am glad it should be a political one. For political crimes, being more affairs of intelligence than other kinds, leave more strongly marked traces, and betray themselves just so much the more easily the more ingeniously planned they are. . . . Anyhow, I have already more than one starting-point, and I think I have found a line of scent. . . .

TATIANA
Really?

TORMASSOV
What's that noise at the garden window? . . . Did you hear? . . .

TATIANA
At the third window? . . . Oh, yes, I

The Cloud That Lifted

know. . . . That is the branch of a tree that taps on the pane. . . . It has given us a shiver more than once already. . . .

Tormassov

There is no wind.

Tatiana

There is always a certain amount of a breeze blowing at this corner of the house giving on the valley.

Tormassov

Yes, I am following up a scent. . . . I'm looking for a man who saw the murderer running away—or one of his accomplices, at any rate. A man who knows him—recognized him . . . and it seems has spoken about it without being willing to give the name. . . . This man has dis-

The Cloud That Lifted

appeared . . . is hiding most likely, but I think I am close on his track. . . . Another person, for whom I am searching also, spoke of some one he had seen prowling round the park on several days together, before the murder. . . . All this will link up and come together and be made clear. . . . Soon I shall manage to lay my hand on the people suspected . . . to bring them to you, to set them face to face with you . . . and you will decide the matter finally; for there was no one but you who saw, in any way that can be called seeing. . . . So that you are the great judge, the only judge. . . . In the mean time I have something stronger than mere hope, and I was counting on telling our poor dear Sonia this latest good news; but since she is still asleep I will come back later. . . . There is nothing, I know there is nothing that

The Cloud That Lifted

can lighten her grief and distress except the prompt and justly merited punishment of the murderer.

TATIANA

She thinks of nothing else now. . . . I don't know her now when she speaks about it . . . so gentle as she always is, so indulgent, so forgiving and kind, she has suddenly become implacable, and only lives to avenge her father. . . .

TORMASSOV

She is right. . . . We must make an example. . . . Good-bye. . . . Tell her . . . no, don't say anything beforehand. I'll come back this evening, and I'll tell her myself. . . . Don't show me out; I know the old house.

> [*He goes out on the left. When* TATIANA *is quite certain he is*

The Cloud That Lifted

gone, she goes and opens one of the French windows in the background. Enter AXEL *very circumspectly.*]

Scene II

[Axel; Tatiana.]

Axel
You are alone? . . .

Tatiana
Yes.

Axel
Where is Sonia? . . .

Tatiana
Asleep.

Axel
How is she? . . .

The Cloud That Lifted

TATIANA

Not very well.

AXEL

What? . . . Not well? . . . Tell me. . . .

TATIANA

Don't be disturbed; the danger is over. . . . Her nerves are greatly shaken, and the doctor was afraid, and is afraid even now, of something wrong with the brain if any new emotions come to give her a fresh shock. . . . She is asleep . . . the first moment of relaxation and rest she has had for five days.

AXEL

Who was that with you?

TATIANA

Tormassov, who is in charge of the in-

The Cloud That Lifted

quiry. . . . We will have to arrange some other signal. . . . He noticed the tapping of the branch on the pane. . . . In any case it is n't possible now for you to come here again. . . . The garden is watched by Tormassov's detectives. . . . I don't even understand how you managed to get into it now without being seen, and you will have to take extraordinary precautions to get out again. . . .

Axel

All right, we 'll see. . . . I must see Sonia.

Tatiana

You shall see her . . . she will call me as soon as she is awake.

Axel

I can't stand it any longer. . . . I

The Cloud That Lifted

have made up my mind. . . . I can't stand it, and it is impossible for me to go on hiding the truth from her. . . . As long as her father's body was here, actually in the house . . . yes . . . there was an excuse, a pretext for silence. . . . And, besides, I was only able to come to her for a moment, and in secret, in the midst of such an agony of despair that every word that might have been said would have been strangled in tears. But now I neither can nor will. . . . When I think that in a moment she will open that door, and that her first movement will be to throw herself into my arms . . . and I . . . No! No . . . it has gone on long enough.

TATIANA
If it means your dealing her this blow, you shall not see her.

The Cloud That Lifted

AXEL
I shall be the judge of that.

TATIANA
You shall not see her until you swear to say nothing to her to-day. . . . I don't ask you to keep the truth hidden from her, but just not to reveal it to her until she is strong enough to hear it.

AXEL
A man and a woman have different ideas as to duty and honesty, and I will not take my cue from a woman.

TATIANA
I know . . . a man, just to be rid of a secret that burdens him, to be able to draw untroubled breath, a man is ready to sacrifice the very life of the thing he loves.

The Cloud That Lifted

AXEL

But just think. . . . I am becoming . . . I am beyond forgiveness; I have no excuse now; I would not deserve to be called a man if I take a single kiss from her before telling her of the dreadful thing that lies between us! . . . I have delayed only too long already! . . . I ought to have cried out the unimaginable truth to her on the night itself! . . . I have no more than just enough strength left to reveal it to her, to go away, to lose all, to disappear and make an end!

TATIANA

It is n't yourself and your position you should be thinking of, but hers. . . . Anyhow, it is quite a simple matter; it depends on me whether you see her or not, and you shall not see her until I have your pledged word.

The Cloud That Lifted

AXEL

Where have you got this determination from, Tatiana; I don't recognize you at all.

TATIANA

I am defending what I love. I am defending the girl who received me in a way no sister in the world could have done . . . who consoled me, encouraged me, brought me back to life from the depths of an unfathomable, unescapable distress . . . to whom I owe everything, even the energy with which I am fighting against you so as to spare her a trial that would kill her. . . .

AXEL

Very well, then, I shall not speak today.

The Cloud That Lifted

TATIANA

[*Holding out her hand to him.*] Thanks; now you prove to me that you know how to love her as she deserves to be loved.

AXEL

In exchange, I insist on something.

TATIANA

What? . . .

AXEL

That you say nothing to her, either; that you must make no allusion and no insinuation under pretext of preparing her mind. . . . She must be told by my mouth, and by no other.

TATIANA

That is clearly understood. . . . And

The Cloud That Lifted

yet before coming to that, I want to tell you everything that is in my mind. . . . We have been friends for a long, long time, Axel. . . . It is nearly three years now, I think, since we first met each other; it was I who brought you and made you know the woman you were to love. . . . Sometimes it seems to me as if I were the elder sister and guardian of that love which I have seen spring up under my eyes. . . . It seems to me that I am the more bound to watch over its happiness since it was not without a pang that I saw it grow and flourish. . . . I can say it to you now, since it is a thing of the past, and passed away. . . . I loved you, Axel, or at least I thought I loved you. . . . As you were in love with our dear Sonia, you never suspected this love of mine that never said a word.

The Cloud That Lifted

AXEL
Tatiana!

TATIANA
Do not pity me; my love is not dead. . . . It has changed its shape, and has bent itself wholly on your happiness, the happiness of you both. . . . My part seems a little sad, but it has its smiling moments; and you could never imagine how sweet it is to be in love with the happiness of those we love, even while that happiness, the more it increases, removes them the further from us. . . .

AXEL
My dear, kind Tatiana! . . .

TATIANA
Let us say no more of these things, which are of so little significance at this mo-

The Cloud That Lifted

ment. . . . This is what I wanted to say to you. . . . It is very difficult, but perhaps you will understand me in a moment.

Axel

Tell me. . . .

Tatiana

You have made up your mind to destroy, and you are on the point of poisoning in its very well springs the most beautiful, the deepest, the most perfect love that any one could ever find. . . . And for what? Merely to obey a first inevitable and instinctive impulse of selfishness, to relieve yourself of a scruple and an anxious thought that you ought to have courage enough to bear singly by yourself till the end of your life.

Axel

Speak more clearly. . . .

The Cloud That Lifted
TATIANA

You have killed Sonia's father, by a mere accident, without knowing it, without intending it; but this death, in all justice and in all conscience, was as far remote from you as if it had come from the fall of a tree or of a rock. You would not blame yourself had you seen the tree fall or the rock crash down; no more should you accuse yourself because a bullet, unintended and astray, struck the person you could not discern in the darkness, and whose mere presence you could not even have suspected. . . . For I was there, remember. . . . I know what I know. . . . I saw what I saw, and I tell myself that in your place I would not say a word, and that I would be strong enough to keep locked away in my own heart that dreadful blunder of chance and the night.

The Cloud That Lifted

AXEL

Tatiana!

TATIANA

Axel? . . .

AXEL

You belong to another race, and that is why I summon up my patience and try to tell myself that you cannot understand. But this must be the last time you say such things to me. . . .

TATIANA

Why? . . .

AXEL

Because I should take such steps as would prevent you from seeing Sonia ever again. . . . Now let us talk of something else. . . . Tormassov has just gone from here; what does he know?

The Cloud That Lifted

TATIANA

Nothing definite. . . . He is hunting for a man who saw the murderer, as they call him, running away, and who it appears has talked about it without being willing to give the name. This man has disappeared, and it is believed that he is hiding. Did you meet with any one in your flight?

AXEL

When I had climbed the wall, I do believe I was seen by some one passing by, some one I do not know, and who, I am quite sure, does not know me either. . . .

TATIANA

Another person whom he is also looking for spoke of an individual that had been seen more than once prowling around the park. . . .

The Cloud That Lifted

AXEL

I take such careful precautions that I have no fears on that score. . . . So, then, there is very little. . . . Did he question you again? . . .

TATIANA

Yes.

AXEL

What did you say to him?

TATIANA

I repeated what I had said at the first questioning, and laid more stress on the idea of an ambush and a political crime, so as to throw him off the scent.

AXEL

That is rather dangerous.

The Cloud That Lifted

TATIANA

No, it's all too vague. . . . I made no clear statement except that I had seen right in front of me, in full light, the man who fired the fatal shot; so that in case of need, if the search should light on you, I should be able to fail to recognize you. . . .

AXEL

He has no suspicion?

TATIANA

About you? . . . All the time you have been coming here secretly into this lonely and deserted garden, nobody, not even a servant, has ever suspected your presence. As for Tormassov, he does n't even know of your existence!

AXEL

Sonia's father never spoke to him about me, then?

The Cloud That Lifted

TATIANA

Sonia's father hardly knew you at all. . . . He had driven you away, once for all, in an explosion of wrath; he never admitted the possibility of any resistance to his will; and so he imagined he had abolished you, and he was too proud and too taciturn ever to speak about it to any one, not even to his oldest friend.

AXEL

And then, in any case, it does n't matter; my judge is Sonia. . . . She will welcome me or send me away; and if she sends me away, I will go and give myself up. . . . Under the dictator's régime we are now enjoying it means execution within twenty-four hours, and that is all I ask. . . .

The Cloud That Lifted

TATIANA

I think I've heard her walking about in her room for some minutes already. . . . [*Listening.*] She has got up. . . . [*Opening the door on the right.*] She is coming down the stairs. . . . Above everything, be careful, and remember your promise.

> [*She goes out to meet* SONIA, *and the next moment comes back with her.*]

Scene III

[Sonia; Tatiana; Axel.]

Sonia

[*Pale with her eyes wide and shining, feverish and shivering.*] Axel! [*To Tatiana in a reproachful tone, while she throws herself into* Axel's *arms.*] And you never let me know! . . .

Tatiana

You were asleep . . . the doctor had forbidden you to be awakened on any pretext whatever. . . .

Sonia

How stupid you all are, everybody that

The Cloud That Lifted

isn't in love! What sleep could be half as good as the presence of the one I find once more and embrace at last! [*To* AXEL.] Have you been here long? . . .

AXEL

No, Tatiana was telling—

SONIA

It is really you, your hands and your very arms, your eyes, your real self come back to me again once more! . . .

AXEL

[*Noticing that she grows pale and totters.*] Sonia! What is the matter?

SONIA

Nothing . . . nothing . . . sometimes I have a passing touch of faintness. . . . Ah! I no longer believed it, and I be-

The Cloud That Lifted

lieved in nothing any more. . . . I could n't imagine your existence and your presence. . . . Where were you? What were you doing? . . . Why did I not see you any more? . . .

AXEL
They told me it was impossible. . . .

SONIA
Who told you that? . . . Why? . . . Because I was weeping? . . . But that was just the time. . . . Ah, yes! I know . . . ah! always to be hiding . . . to meet like wrong-doers, all because of the hate that fed and fostered this crime. Ah, I am tired of it all! . . . disgusted, sickened! . . . Now it's all over . . . there will be no more struggles, no more parties, no more country, no more intrigues. . . . I will have no more of all

The Cloud That Lifted

these about me. . . . I won't have them, I tell you! . . . Ah! I have paid my share, and I have paid yours, too! . . . Now it is enough; do you not think it is enough, Axel? . . . Yes, and to prove it you shall take up my duty, my appointed task. Oh, without betraying your own folk! . . . But this unparalled stroke at last gives us the right to think only of ourselves . . . the old duties are dead and gone; there remains only one and you can take it up, for beyond the others it is a duty of simple justice, which even the bitterest enemies may join in loving! . . . I have never hated before, but this time I hate! . . . and you hate with me! Tell me you do; you must, for I need you, and I need to be helped.

AXEL

Sonia! . . .

The Cloud That Lifted

SONIA

Yes! Yes! Yes! . . . one might think you do not feel it as yet. I can understand that you have not pondered day and night as I have . . . you will see . . . but to be able to love we must know how to hate. Imagine the man that committed this outrage going away quietly and peacefully, free and proud through life, as though it was nothing! . . . Ah, no, no! . . . I am in his path, and you will be in his path, too! . . . If others forget him, we will never forget. . . . We will seek and search everywhere, for years if need be, but we will find the track. . . . I am all for men avenging their wrongs. . . . Yes, we can forgive when it is ourselves . . . though there is too much forgiving in the world . . . but the wrong done to those we love—not that, never! . . .

AXEL

Sonia, calm yourself . . . you are growing terribly excited; you are beside yourself; and you are doing yourself harm.

SONIA

I am not excited; I am easing my grief, relieving my hate. . . . This is the first time I have been allowed to speak. I have been choking, stifling, do you hear? . . . You know what there is to know? . . .

AXEL

Tatania has told me.

SONIA

It was never one of your people that

The Cloud That Lifted

could have done it. That is impossible; I am certain of it! . . . It is too ugly, too cowardly! . . . What do you think? . . .

Axel

I think with you that none of my people . . . but there are others. . . .

Sonia

No! . . . no! . . . I was sure of it. . . . And, then, you have told me twenty times over that neither you nor your people ever employed such means to pull down an enemy. . . . No, no, the people who are near you could never do that. . . . There is no shadow of doubt, it was an ambush and an assassination.

Axel

That is not proved. . . . It might also

The Cloud That Lifted

have been by chance, perhaps some mistake. . . .

SONIA
A mistake! . . . a chance! . . . what a pure chance it must be that brings the traitor sneaking like that into the victim's garden! . . . and the bullet in the neck and the gang in their places!

AXEL
A gang in their places? . . . There was never any question of—

SONIA
Ask Tatiana. . . . Is n't that so? you are sure there were five or six.

TATIANA
Five or six, I don't know. . . . I'm not sure about anything, since I could see nothing.

The Cloud That Lifted

SONIA

No, but anyhow you believe—

TATIANA

I did get the impression that in fact several persons—

SONIA

[*To* AXEL.] But you, what have you heard? . . . Tatiana told me you were searching eagerly and that you already had found a scent.

AXEL

I did n't say that . . . I am still only dealing with the vaguest hints and signs.

SONIA

No matter, what are they? . . . You must neglect nothing. . . . You have a better chance than Tormassov or any one

The Cloud That Lifted

else to discover the truth. . . . Everybody speaks freely before you . . . no one has any mistrust. . . . Let us see now. . . . What motive? . . . Is it a political crime? . . . But no, that you would know. . . . And it was not for robbery . . . so then it was for revenge . . . a personal revenge. . . . Come, what do you know about it? . . . Why do you say nothing? . . .

Axel

I will tell you what I know when I have anything certain. . . .

Sonia

But no . . . do not let us fold our arms and wait for certainties. . . . They never come in that way; that is how they escape us. . . . Let us take everything that offers . . . that is real certainty!

The Cloud That Lifted

Why these reticences? . . . Do you not venture to speak before Tatiana? . . . My dearest Tatiana! See her clear, fresh face! She was my one only refuge in these days of weeping, and she talked to me about you. [*To* TATIANA.] But indeed and indeed, I understand, he would rather see me alone. You must know that in spite of everything you are a third person, and he does not know yet that we are but one heart, you and I.

> [TATIANA *goes out.* SONIA *staggers to the divan and sinks down on it.* AXEL *runs to her and holds her in his arms.*]

Scene IV

[Axel; Sonia.]

Axel

Sonia! . . . you are all pale . . . your hands are burning and trembling. . . . Come into my arms, my poor darling Sonia. . . . You are altogether worn out, and indeed you are wrong to be so excited. . . . Tatiana tells me the doctor is uneasy and insists that you are to rest and not to think about . . .

Sonia

It's nothing. . . . I am better . . . it is just a little fatigue and the remains of my fever. . . . It's my nerves recovering

The Cloud That Lifted

from the strain. But there now . . . I am born again. . . . The best rest is in your arms; that was what I was waiting for, and that is my one cure. . . . Ah, I needed them as one might need shade on a burning desert. . . . I need your calm and your steadfast loyalty, and your mere presence has brought me back to life, already. . . . I was calling, calling you without ceasing, and you never came at all. . . .

Axel

But indeed I did; I came at the very first moment; only you seemed not to see me or hear me. . . .

Sonia

At the first moment. . . . Ah! I no longer knew who came or who went. . . . For an instant I thought really that my

The Cloud That Lifted

reason was oozing away from every part of my body. I no longer dared to speak, to listen, to look. I felt that my life, that my whole being no longer held to anything. But you cannot understand, you could never understand the wrong, the injury that I have suffered, and what I have lost. . . . He was not a father like other fathers: a simple, kind old man, indulgent, attentive. . . .

AXEL
Come, my darling Sonia, you are tiring yourself still more, instead of resting quietly, quietly in my arms. . . . Let us have done with these memories that kindle your anguish afresh.

SONIA
No, no, they soothe it, they calm it. . . . I must speak of it, and all I say of

The Cloud That Lifted

it helps to bring me back to peace. . . . You did not know him. . . . You never saw him except that once when he was angry. . . . But you would have loved him. . . . He looked forbidding and terrifying to any one that did n't know. . . . People thought he was reserved, passionate, tyrannical; they could see his sudden violent fits of rage. . . . His rage was often blind, it is quite true . . . but it was his strength seeking some outlet, and it was all quickly forgotten in such kindly regrets. . . . They said his ideas were narrow and obstinate and out of date, but what of that? . . . He thought he was serving his master and Holy Russia. . . . And after all it was a great idea, that idea, too. . . . I never approved it, but I admired his faithfulness. . . . You, you serve another idea, and I do not judge you. . . . But why should men hate one another because they follow two paths that are not the same? . . . But you would have loved him, and he would have loved you. . . . And he understood everything, he lit up everything, he soared above everything he did. . . . I adored you in him. . . . I love him still in you. . . . If my arms clasp you like this, in spite of my grief, if I can give you kisses through my tears, it is because his memory—

Axel

No . . . no . . .

Sonia

What! . . . You push me away! . . . What is it? . . .

Axel

I am not pushing you away, but I want

The Cloud That Lifted

to change the course of these thoughts that give you so much pain. . . .

SONIA

But no, they are doing me good. . . . So you don't understand that they are necessary to me, and that I would stifle if they did not pour out of my bursting heart. . . . It is by thinking of all he was to me that I imagine myself once more in possession of what I have lost. . . . I drew from him even in my very childhood as one might draw from a spring that is always full and never ruffled or turbid. . . . He was never a mere father. . . . A father! an easy word to say . . . and yet the word means nothing unless it means everything. . . . He was my friend, my brother in every game, in every smile, the sage of every day and every thought.

The Cloud That Lifted

... Ah! if you had known. ... How strange it is that some one has to be dead for us to see him at last in all his true reality! ... He thought he hated you and wished you ill, and he thought, too, that you detested him. ... That makes you smile. ...

Axel

No. ...

Sonia

You have forgiven him? ...

Axel

Yes. ...

Sonia

He was so whole-heartedly inflexible; when I spoke of you to him, he went into a wild rage! He said that never should

The Cloud That Lifted

the worst enemy of the Czar, one of the heads of the band that is keeping Finland in turmoil . . . he said that rather than give his daughter to one of the brigands who . . . well, I don't know what he said. . . . And on my side I was amused; I felt so sure in reality, and I smiled at him and I smiled at you. . . . A few more days, I said to my own self, a few weeks longer, and they will come together, they will get to know each other and they will adore each other. . . . I was in no impatient hurry; I was not uneasy; it was inevitably certain. You were bound to love each other, since I loved you both. . . . If he had been your father you could not have been more like him in everything he was to those who knew his heart and his ideas. . . . When I see you there, and the more I look at you. . . .

The Cloud That Lifted

Look me in the face. . . . Why do you drop your eyes? . . . One might say that you bear him a grudge still.

AXEL

No, but I think if I had known him better this dreadful thing might possibly never have happened!

SONIA

Why? . . .

AXEL

I don't know. . . . One never knows. . . . Often the smallest movement, the slightest chance alters a whole destiny.

SONIA

Perhaps, yes, who knows? . . . He would have been there, between us two, to-day or to-morrow. . . . His smile will

The Cloud That Lifted

always be something lacking to my happiness. . . . A father's smile upon his daughter's love is a powerful charm against fear or mischance. . . . I am looking at you again. . . . Like you, he had so clear, so transparent a face that the smallest thought held back and not disclosed filled it with anguish and reproach. In him I could see everything, just as I could see in you if you ever wished to hide anything from me. . . . And to think that all this—by one single stupid blow . . . without excuse, without reason . . . I am not a cruel woman . . . I have found forgiveness for everything . . . but not for this, never, never! . . . I would shatter the branch, I would grind the stone to powder that had stricken him by chance; whatever was the motive, whoever was the doer of the deed nothing can

The Cloud That Lifted

ever excuse it. . . . We will find him.
. . . I dedicate my life to the task; you
will help me, will you not? You will
throw into it all your ardour, your
strength, your courage; you will give up
everything else, think of nothing but him;
and our sweetest kisses will unite in the
love that seeks for justice.

[*Enter* TATIANA.]

Scene V

[Axel; Sonia; Tatiana.]

Tatiana

Tormassov is coming back . . . he is crossing the park. [*To* Axel.] Go and hide.

Sonia

Why? . . . There is nothing to conceal now. . . . What other people think is nothing to us here any more. . . . I will introduce Axel to him.

Tatiana

No, no, not to-day. . . . Believe me, it will be better not. . . . There are reasons . . . you shall hear them later. . . . Is n't that so, Axel? . . . I hear him coming. . . .

Axel
I will wait out in the park. . . .

Tatiana
No, don't trust the park. . . . Here . . . here.

> [*She makes* Axel *go out by the door on the right, and goes with him, coming back towards the end of the scene between* Tormassov *and* Sonia. *Enter* Tormassov *by the door on the left.*]

Scene VI

[Tormassov; Sonia; *then* Tatiana.]

Tormassov
[*Entering.*] So there you are, up and about, Sonia? . . . How are you? I have good news, great news.

Sonia
What is it?

Tormassov
If it is true, and I think it is, that an invisible power brings the murderer back to the scene of his crime, ours is taken.

Sonia
No? . . . How? . . . Where is he?

The Cloud That Lifted

TORMASSOV

Here, most likely. . . . The man has been seen prowling among the shubberies in the avenue and then climbing the wall of the garden. . . . I have had the park surrounded. . . . He is taken in the net. . . . Now we have to put our hand on his person. . . . We are going to beat the grounds systematically for him. . . . I have my men.

SONIA

I will be your guide.
[*They go out.*]

CURTAIN

ACT II

The same scene. Next morning

ACT II

Scene I

[Sonia; Tatiana.]

Tatiana

[*Comes up to* Sonia, *places herself on the edge of the arm-chair in which the latter is sitting, and puts her arm tenderly about her neck.*] You seem very quiet and calm this morning, my big Sonia; your cheeks are getting back their beautiful clear colour. What a nice thing you are to kiss like this!

Sonia

[*Kissing her in turn.*] You too, you

The Cloud That Lifted

are nice . . . it is like drinking the dew of the morning . . . all crystal, azure, rosy, dewy, dawn-like. . . . Yes, I feel myself stronger and almost rested in spite of the emotions of last night. . . . I slept like a good little child, and I almost reproach myself a little for that, for indeed nature and life, if we let them, would be in such dreadful haste to forget our most tragical despairs. . . .

Tatiana

I was so afraid that last night's alarm and that fruitless pursuit in the park, these fresh emotions just as you were recovering from your fever attack, might have made us lose all that five days of healing tears had done to overcome your anguish. . . . I love you so tenderly and so deeply, my big Sonia. . . . I owe you so many, many things; and I know so well

The Cloud That Lifted

that I shall never have anything to give you but my kisses, the kisses of a harmless little sister. . . .

Sonia

A little sister who has saved me from the shadows. . . . You have been so good, so devoted through these long black days when I would have been lost without one gleam of light if you had not been there.

Tatiana

You know the doctor was very uneasy about you last night. . . . He was afraid of . . . what is it? . . . a brain fever . . . and then I don't know what all—I've forgotten the name. . . . And our good Tormassov was in despair when he heard how stupid he had been and how dangerous it was to subject you to any

The Cloud That Lifted

great excitement. . . . I hadn't been able to warn him. . . . He was so happy over his good news; he thought he had the guilty person in his hands, and his zeal is so immense. . . .

SONIA

Yes, his zeal touches me. . . . He adored my father. . . . But I think he is full of very simple-minded illusions. . . . He has remained faithful to ancient methods that suppose a murderer must needs come and parade about the scene of his crime every night. . . . We are no longer at that point. . . . We are dealing here with something far more advanced. . . . Axel and myself, we shall have to come to his help, or else our enemy will be at large for a long time yet. . . . But I have no fears. . . . From this very day I am setting to work, and I can't tell why, but something tells me I am near my goal. . . .

TATIANA
Shall I tell you? . . . I know why the murderer got away last night. . . .

SONIA
How? . . .

TATIANA
Because he was n't in the garden at all. . . .

SONIA
You thought of that on the spot, without help or trying? . . . But we must take note of it. . . . You would make a wonderful examining magistrate. . . .

TATIANA
No, it is n't what you think, and I have

The Cloud That Lifted

hardly the heart to make fun. . . . But I don't know what ought to be done, and I wish you were in my place.

Sonia

Your preamble discloses serious torment at heart; it will presently give birth to some terrible and playful enigma, some huge and innocent scruple. It came last night direct from your moon-country, where the babies are lovely but a little unruly. Come, now; let us have the monster. . . . We shall know at once if it has solid ribs, or if, like so many others, it turns into dew at the first cockcrow. . . .

Tatiana

I am not brave enough to tell it you this morning. . . . You seem so happy, so sure of the future.

The Cloud That Lifted

SONIA

I am not happy, but full of confidence, and a strength that I do not recognize sustains and shines on me. . . .

TATIANA

You see. . . . It will be better for me to remain silent. . . .

SONIA

Come, I will help you along. . . . I am sure it is still the old phantom returning, that you have found it again in the depths of your heart . . . that you love Axel still? . . .

TATIANA

No! . . .

SONIA

No! it's not that now? . . . Have

The Cloud That Lifted

you lost your ring, or your pearl necklace? . . . Come, help me to it then; I've nothing else to suggest, I tell you. . . .

TATIANA

First of all I want to ask your advice. . . .

SONIA

What, again? I give you advice every day; what do you do with it, and what becomes of all my monitions? . . . I have never found the slightest hint or trace of them in your life. . . . You receive them with a smile, like beautiful flowers whose perfume one breathes in for a moment, and which are then left to lie forgotten on the table. . . . And upon my word it's the wisest thing to do with them. . . . And, anyway, what does it matter? . . . my garden of counsels is all but inexhaustible . . . I have ten thousand left that will never be taken. . . . But what is it this time? . . .

TATIANA
This time I will follow your advice at once. . . .

SONIA
That's the way, in the very moment I give it to you, for fear it might evaporate like all the others; for I think that too fine counsellings have subtle perfumes that don't linger for as much as a moment.

TATIANA
Don't go on laughing, I beg you, Sonia . . . this is so grave and so sad. . . .

SONIA
Come, I am serious, since you are so

grave. You know well enough that I am only laughing like this to cheat my tears. . . . Now, then, come to me and kiss me; I am listening and I love you dearly. . . .

SONIA

No, I can't say it and kiss you at the same time. . . .

SONIA

Well, then, say it to me without kissing me. . . . But indeed you are making me uneasy; you have never been very long before unfolding your dreams and your fairy-tales. . . . It is something very dreadful then? . . .

TATIANA

Yes. . . .

The Cloud That Lifted

SONIA
Well, then? . . .

TATIANA
Well, then! What would you do if you knew a thing that nobody knows . . . that you are the only person, absolutely the single only one person who knows. . . . A frightful thing, and one utterly beyond belief. . . . A thing that must infallibly destroy the happiness of all you love best in the whole world.

SONIA
Good God! What is it? . . . and what is this enigma? . . . First of all I would begin by thinking that such a thing cannot exist, except only in the imagination of a small girl who has been reading novels her mother forgot and left lying about on a garden seat. . . .

The Cloud That Lifted

TATIANA
It does exist, nevertheless. . . .

SONIA
Well, then, what? . . . I don't seem to recognize your eyes. . . . Is it about him? . . . Is it about me? . . .

TATIANA
What would you do? . . . You are the one that must decide. . . .

SONIA
But I'll decide anything you wish, provided only you will tell it me. . . . Please to say clearly what you mean. . . . How can you expect any one to give you advice if she does not know all the circumstances. . . . The most trifling circumstance can throw the course of the greatest of duties off the track.

The Cloud That Lifted

TATIANA

I will tell you. . . . Why should I speak? . . . Why should I be silent? . . .

SONIA

Well, then? . . .

TATIANA

It is you who are concerned in it. . . .

SONIA

Ah! . . .

TATIANA

And he. . . .

SONIA

Ah! . . . at last! . . . And so much the better! . . . If it concerns us both, I am reassured. . . .

The Cloud That Lifted

TATIANA

Don't talk like that; I would never have the strength if you do. . . .

SONIA

Come, come then, I'm listening.

TATIANA

Does anybody forgive the one that discloses a misfortune beyond compare? . . .

SONIA

Yes, yes! . . . I tell you yes! . . . But what has happened? . . . Axel is n't hurt? . . . ill? . . . No? . . . What is it, then? . . . What is it? . . .

TATIANA

I know who killed your father. . . .

SONIA

Who? . . . You? . . . When? . . . Since when? . . . But you have twenty

The Cloud That Lifted

times told me you did n't know . . .
that you had seen nothing, and that it was
black night, all darkness. . . . And now
you come and tell me—

TATIANA
It is now you must believe me. . . .

SONIA
Well, then, be it so; no matter; but who
is it, who is it? . . .

TATIANA
It was he! . . .

SONIA
He! . . . What he? . . .

TATIANA
Axel! . . .

The Cloud That Lifted

SONIA

Axel!... Ah, Axel!... Don't look at me so stupefied because I am smiling; I know, I know that anything can be expected when one is talking with you. Between you and me that is of no great consequence, and everybody knows that dreams and realities dance such rounds in your childish head ... that when the dance is done you no longer know yourself what is true or false.... Between you and me it is all very well, and we may amuse ourselves with it, but in other times and in other circumstances you ought to be careful; the game might not be without its dangers.... But come; let us talk about something else.... Where did you put away the letter Tormassov's secretary sent me this morning?...

The Cloud That Lifted

TATIANA

Perhaps you will believe it if he tells you so himself?

SONIA

If he tells me what? . . .

TATIANA

That he killed your father. . . .

SONIA

Who? . . . Axel? . . . If he tells me so himself? . . . Certainly, I will believe it . . . and I am curious, as a matter of fact, very curious. . . . But why did you not tell me this on the night itself? . . .

TATIANA

Because I was struggling . . . because it was too hideously terrible . . .

The Cloud That Lifted

because I hoped always that he would tell you himself as he had promised to do. . . .

SONIA
Ah! . . . he had promised? . . .

TATIANA
Yes. . . .

SONIA
And why has he not done so? . . .

TATIANA
I am afraid he would never be brave enough. . . .

SONIA
He! never be brave enough? . . . But you don't know then. . . . But I am absurd. . . . I am asking questions, discuss-

ing, arguing, as if I was really beginning to believe. . . . Yet I know you . . . and the fairy world in which you spend your life, a world all full of incoherencies. . . . But you are so serious, so sincere . . . and so full of conviction with your big eyes, as clear as those of a child telling its mother it has seen God, that one always lets oneself be caught and taken in. . . . So, then, all you had told us till this moment was not true? . . .

TATIANA

Everything I have said is true, except when I said I did n't know who fired the shot. . . .

SONIA

And it was he? . . . You saw him? . . .

The Cloud That Lifted

TATIANA
Yes. . . .

SONIA
You said it was black as pitch. . . .

TATIANA
The moon shone out now and then. . . .

SONIA
Who fired first? . . . There were six reports? . . .

TATIANA
There were several of them, but Axel fired—

SONIA
Where was he? . . .

The Cloud That Lifted

TATIANA

Behind a tree. . . . You know it, the big dead tree. . . .

SONIA

In hiding! . . . He was waiting, then. . . . He was on the watch! . . .

TATIANA

He looked as if he was waiting. . . .

SONIA

And my father? . . . What did he do? . . .

TATIANA

He fired, too. . . .

SONIA

The others did n't fire? . . .

The Cloud That Lifted

TATIANA

No, when your father fell, they took to flight. . . .

SONIA

And Axel? . . .

TATIANA

He ran away, too. . . .

SONIA

He knows you recognized him? . . .

TATIANA

Yes.

SONIA

You have spoken to him about it since? . . .

TATIANA

Yes. . . .

The Cloud That Lifted

SONIA

And he means to confess to me? . . .

TATIANA

I told him that if he did n't tell you I would tell you myself.

SONIA

And then? . . .

TATIANA

He implored me to say nothing, declaring that it was all chance . . . that he was in self-defence . . . that he had never meant . . . that he was not guilty.

SONIA

[*Angrily.*] You are lying, but I am stupid. . . . When is he coming? . . .

TATIANA

He is waiting for me to call him. . . .

The Cloud That Lifted

SONIA

Where is he? . . .

TATIANA

He has spent the night in the empty pavilion. . . . I hid him there while Tormassov's police were beating the garden. . . .

SONIA

What cumbersome mysteries in everything you do! . . . This must come to an end. . . . I laugh once more. . . . I am searching in my mind. . . . I have already seen glimmerings of something suspicious in you . . . a crowd of little traits in your transparent limpid nature that now rise up to explain many things to me. . . . But no, it is n't possible . . . but no, it is too wild . . . too stupid or too malignant. . . .

The Cloud That Lifted

TATIANA

[*Bursting into tears.*]   Sonia!

SONIA

Call Axel.

[TATIANA *goes out on the right. Left alone,* SONIA *mechanically goes to the mirror, arranges some small objects, etc. The door on right opens. Enter* AXEL.]

Scene II

[Sonia; Axel.]

Sonia
[*Throwing herself on* Axel's *neck.*] Axel! . . .

Axel
Sonia! . . . how is it with you? . . . I could n't shut so much as an eye, I was so disturbed by the state I had seen you in last night, so pale, so nervous, so weary and fever-stricken. . . .

Sonia
And I, too, I could never have slept if I had known that you were out there, in

The Cloud That Lifted

that room without a bed, without a fire, without a light, a victim to the childish folly of Tatiana. And you submitted to her like an obedient child? . . .

AXEL

The garden was overrun with Tormassov's police. I wanted to spare you anything like a scandal.

SONIA

Have you found out nothing fresh? . . .

AXEL

How could I have found out anything? . . . I have not been out of the house? . . .

SONIA

I have learned something important. . . .

The Cloud That Lifted

AXEL
How? . . . from whom? . . .

SONIA
From Tatiana. . . .

AXEL
What was it? . . .

SONIA
Have you no idea of it? . . .

AXEL
I don't know. . . . I am trying to read in your face to understand why you are smiling. . . .

SONIA
She says it was you who killed my father. . . .

The Cloud That Lifted

AXEL

What? . . . and she has just told me . . . she has just been begging me—

SONIA

She is quite mad; we know that. . . .

AXEL

Not mad . . . but—

SONIA

What? . . .

AXEL

Since she has spoken, I must not keep silence any longer. . . . She has told the truth. . . .

SONIA

How? . . .

AXEL

Yes, it was I. . . .

The Cloud That Lifted

SONIA
You! . . .

AXEL
I . . . without intending it . . . without knowing! . . .

SONIA
I do not believe . . . I can't believe you . . .

AXEL
[*Coming to her.*] Sonia! . . .

SONIA
[*Springing back from him.*] Ah! don't come near me! . . . no! no! . . . don't come forward and don't touch me! . . . It is n't possible! . . . You could never have been able to come like this . . . talk to me, kiss me, without re-

The Cloud That Lifted

coiling with shame or crying out the truth in my face. . . . Or then! . . . Oh! then! But no, this is only a dream or some dreadful trial. . . . I cannot see the meaning . . . it is a gust of madness passing—over both of you . . . and trying to sweep me along with it, too. . . . An abominable game! . . . What! . . . the one being I love and could love among all the millions of others that might have done it! . . . He is there before my eyes! . . . coldly lying in wait! . . . No, no, whatever any one may say . . . things like that do not happen, will never happen. . . . But tell me then that it is not true before I fall! . . . Tell me it is all a mockery of my grief, of anything you please . . . I am ready to believe anything, I am ready to understand anything you may say . . . but not that! in God's name! not that . . .

The Cloud That Lifted

Axel

That is the one thing dreadfully true. . . .

Sonia

But then everything is all true! . . . But then what? . . . what then? . . . What do you want? . . . What are you waiting for? . . . If you come back here, it is to hunt for death. . . . I have only to arm myself now with any weapons, no matter what, anything I find to hand . . . then it is to brave me, to look at horror, terror, madness rising up in my eyes and bursting my bosom. . . . No! . . . No! . . . it is n't that! . . . There are limits to everything, even to things beyond imagining. . . . I must reason with myself; I must control myself! . . . I will not let myself be overthrown like this by the madness that is ravening round my reason. . . .

No! . . . No! . . . I can see very well. . . . There is a mistake, some misapprehension! What do I know? . . . Such things happen, too. . . . We know that everything can happen. . . . But speak, then, answer, and don't stay there like the loud confession incarnate of what ought to be denied.

Axel

I cannot deny. . . . It is the only way in which I can expiate a fearful mischance. . . .

Sonia

Let us think! . . . let us think, while there is still time! [*Taking her head between her hands.*] For I feel something

The Cloud That Lifted

breaking away here! . . . You that I had chosen! You who, the night before the deed, were so full of hope, of smiles, of plans for happiness, in which my father's name continually entered, to make the victory of our love the brighter! . . . You who even last night dared to come here, to talk to me of other things, to take my hands in those same hands that. . . . No! . . . No! . . . I must know. . . . Above all things let us know everything! . . . and after that we shall see. . . . How did you kill him? . . .

Axel

You are right. . . . It must needs be told. . . . I was in the garden. . . . I was waiting for you as on the other evenings. . . . I did not know you were away. . . . Your father and Tatiana came out from the house and came down into the park! . . .

Sonia

You recognized them? . . .

Axel

Alas, I did not! I knew afterwards. . . . I hid behind the trees. . . . A piece of dead wood crackles under my foot. . . . Your father hears the noise . . . turns round . . . sees my shadow, no doubt . . . says two or three words that I do not catch; and, without adding more, fires a revolver in my direction.

Sonia

That very morning he had received a letter threatening him with death.

The Cloud That Lifted

Axel

I run away. . . . He follows me. . . . I arrive at the corner made by the two outer walls of the garden. . . . He fires again, two shots that miss me, though the flame of the explosion grazes my cheek. . . . Thrust against the wall, not knowing who is hunting me like this . . . thinking I have to deal with one of Tormassov's policemen, who have been tracking me for several days, I in my turn, in defence of my life, almost without aim, I fire three times with my revolver. . . . At the third shot, the shadow, quite close up to me, utters a cry of distress and falls. . . . I lean over him. . . . A beam strikes down from the moon, as bright as day. . . . I recognize your father. . . . Tatiana runs up, sees me, knows me. . . . She calls out for help,

The Cloud That Lifted

and in a low tone implores me to fly. . . .
It is dreadful; it's stupid . . . it's incredible . . . but that's the whole story.

SONIA

Why did you tell me nothing last night? . . .

AXEL

I had come to confess to you. . . .
Tatiana implored me, ordered me to say nothing. . . .

SONIA

Tatiana! . . .

AXEL

Yes, on account of your health, the dangerous attack the doctor was afraid of . . .

The Cloud That Lifted

Sonia
When were you going to speak? . . .

Axel
Alas! . . . as soon as you were strong enough to bear it! . . .

Sonia
Of your own free will! . . . .

Axel
Sonia! . . .

Sonia
I am at a loss, I am seeking . . . I cannot see two steps in front of me. . . . But if you concealed from me the thing that you came to tell me, is that all? Are you not, for the same reason, hiding something worse from me? . . .

Axel
Worse! . . . What do you mean? . . .

The Cloud That Lifted

Sonia

You killed him then unintentionally, and in defence of your own life? . . . by chance, without knowing . . . without seeing? . . .

Axel

Yes. If it were otherwise would I be here before you?

Sonia

Others who have told the first true tale now add another to it. . . .

Axel

I do not follow clearly. . . .

Sonia

Were you alone in the garden? . . .

The Cloud That Lifted

AXEL

You know that Tatiana is the only one who shares our secret. . . .

SONIA

Your accomplices were seen. . . .

AXEL

My accomplices! . . .

SONIA

Why had you a weapon? . . .

AXEL

Alas, I have good reason to be armed; we must go armed always! . . .

SONIA

And how did you know that he was going to pass that way, near that dead tree, where you could best strike him from behind? . . . For how many nights had you been watching your opportunity?

Axel

How many nights? . . . You know so well that I came every night, and that he hardly ever came down into the garden. . . . Strike him from behind! What do you mean? . . . What do you suspect me of? . . . What is all this? . . .

Sonia

"What do you mean? . . . What is all this?" Aye, this is how one speaks, this is how a man would speak though he were lying from the depth of his soul. . . . That proves nothing; the proof is in ourselves. . . . Look at me, and I am sure. . . . How astonished you are, and how

The Cloud That Lifted

you would smile, if the hour was not such a sad one! . . .

> [*She takes a step toward* Axel *who holds out his arms to her, but at the moment when their hands are about to touch, she draws back with a sharp, instinctive, irresistible movement.*]

Ah no! . . . no! I can't! . . . I don't know when . . . I don't know when! . . . But I love you and I weep. . . . And I long to die and I am almost happy. . . . [*She bursts into sobbing.*]

Axel
What is it, Sonia; will you not tell me? . . .

Sonia
Nothing. . . . Something very big, and

The Cloud That Lifted

then very little things that we shall laugh at together, when we come to weep less. . . . I will call Tatiana so that she may see her work. [*She opens the door on the right and calls.*]

Tatiana, you may come in.

[*Then she comes back beside* AXEL.

. . . TATIANA *appears and pauses on the threshold.*]

Look at us, Tatiana; misfortune will have to find another way.

CURTAIN

ACT III

The same scene. The evening of the same day.

ACT III

Scene I

[Sonia; Tatiana.]

Sonia

Come here, Tatiana. . . . What you have just done is sheer madness, simply inconceivable . . . not to use other words that would be more cruel and more accurate. I have n't even spoken to Axel about your insensate fabrications, it seemed so ridiculous to set his version and yours one against the other. But now that we are alone together, you and I, I wish to hear what made you do such a thing. . . . In spite of everything, there may perhaps be a reason or excuse that I do not perceive even a glimpse of. . . .

The Cloud That Lifted

TATIANA

What is it I have done? . . .

SONIA

Come, come, let us not play at being innocents, and let us have done once for all with those crystal limpid looks that deceive nobody any longer. . . . Axel has told me the truth, and there is no need to repeat it to you, since you know it as well as he does. . . . Why did you work up that monstrous tale of yours? . . . For, if it comes to that, even madness itself has a kind of logicality that guides it and that is always possible to discover. . . .

TATIANA

It is quite possible, Sonia, that I was mistaken about certain details. . . . The night was inky black, and I could not see everything. . . .

The Cloud That Lifted

SONIA
What was it you told Tormassov? . . .

TATIANA
I told him the truth . . . just what I told you . . . just what I shall have to tell everybody. . . . The whole truth, except that I said not a word about Axel. . . .

SONIA
I was still in hope that there was some mistake, some misunderstanding; some slip of the mind, some aberration. . . . But no, I see that it is all clearly determined and planned. . . . But why is this, Tatiana? . . . Will you tell me why? . . . Is it a trap you have set for our love? . . . Some unnecessary, absurd test? . . . A woman's vengeance? . . . For I am enough of a woman myself to know

The Cloud That Lifted

that we have no need of any motive for vengeance to make us avenge ourselves most horribly. . . . Were you reckoning then on sowing distrust and hatred between me and Axel? . . .

Tatiana

I can easily understand that you have no mind to believe me, Sonia . . . but you ought to put this question to yourself, you who are always so just and fair-minded, which of us, Axel or myself, has the greater interest in not telling the whole truth. . . .

Sonia

Come, Tatiana; you know me; you ought to know me. We have lived so long like sisters together. . . . We are alone now with each other, and you know as well as I do that women among them-

The Cloud That Lifted

selves make no mistakes on these deep matters, and that we always know when there is a lie and when the truth passes between us. . . . Now I find it not possible to believe. . . . I am keeping calm still . . . I don't even bear you a grudge for it . . . I am looking for some ray of innocent simplicity . . . of madness even, if necessary, to try to explain a thing that could only be explained by . . . by something that is wholly impossible. . . . What is it you want? . . . What do you expect, and what have you in mind to do? . . .

TATIANA
What have I in my mind to do? . . .

SONIA
Yes. . . . What do you mean me to do myself? . . . You know perfectly well

The Cloud That Lifted

that if you persist in your abominable lying tale it is impossible for you to go on living here any longer and meeting every day the man you are accusing. . . .

Tatiana

You are going to turn me away if I don't tell a lie? . . . Is that the bargain? . . . Very well, since that is to be the price of the truth, I will tell the whole truth. . . .

Sonia

How? . . .

Tatiana

Tormassov is coming to-night? . . .

Sonia

Yes, he is. . . . Why? . . .

The Cloud That Lifted

TATIANA
Because before I leave you both I shall have a word to say to him.

SONIA
No. . . .

TATIANA
Yes, I have not the reasons you have for sparing a murderer. . . .

SONIA
Tatiana! . . . You shall not! . . .

TATIANA
Why should I not, indeed? . . . Is it not my duty? . . . Ah, you have often and often talked to me about duties. . . . Above everything we must be just, and even supposing you did not think he killed your father . . . as I have said . . . it

The Cloud That Lifted

is quite certain, since he confesses to it himself, it is certain that he did kill him. . . . That does n't change the truth at all, and it is n't my intention, before I disappear—for one day I shall disappear—I won't have it happen that punishment should fall on an innocent man through my failing in my duty.

Sonia

You shall not do this as long as I am here. . . .

Tatiana

And how will you stop me?

Sonia

You monster or mad woman! . . . I don't know which! . . . or both together . . . yes, both, for madness by itself could never come to such an infamous

The Cloud That Lifted

thing! . . . So it was hatred then, and envy, and evil that you were storing away behind your virgin looks, your child's smile? . . . But no! that's impossible! . . . but no, it is insensate! . . . When I think of the moments when you were so bright, so transparent . . . when you would tell me everything, and I would tell everything to you! . . . You loved me; I loved you! . . . I welcomed you here like a sister in distress. . . . You told me over and over that I had given you back your courage to go on living. . . . Did I not try everything I could do to ease your grief, to give you fresh confidence in the future? . . . What more could I do? . . . Did I not give you everything that any one could give to the sweetest, the tenderest friend? . . . What can you have against me to punish

The Cloud That Lifted

me like this? . . . What unintended slight? . . . What kindness omitted? . . .

TATIANA

Yes . . . let us speak of kindnesses. . . . I will remind you of the greatest one of all, the best of all. . . . How was is that you came to know Axel? . . . Who brought him to you? . . . Who took him from me, knowing that I loved him? . . . Since you are so fond of crushing us from the lofty heights of your justice, you ought to find it perfectly just that I should take him back from you. . . .

SONIA

Be fair, Tatiana; be straight! . . . When Axel told me that he did not love you, that he had never loved you, that he could never love you, I would still never

The Cloud That Lifted

have thought of giving myself up to his love if you yourself had not declared a hundred times that you loved him no longer, that you felt all too well that he was not for you . . . that we must all submit to the fates that are involved in love. . . .

TATIANA

He was not for me because you had taken him from me! . . . Because you had everything to turn aside the love that was still uncertain of itself: you had wealth, power, beauty with more guile and guile with less ingenuousness. . . . And I, had nothing but what you were willing to leave me, out of a treacherous pity, which itself became the fairest ornament of the love you had filched from a tongue-tied defenceless child! . . . Ah, I have suffered enough! . . . and I have wept

The Cloud That Lifted

enough of the tears you always tenderly feigned not to see, the better to gloat over your triumph! . . . Ah! . . . I have lain long enough with all the weight of my silence and too loyal resignation upon my too just hate that was always longing to leap up and shriek the odious truth into your face! . . . And I would have gone on being cowardly, gone on being stupid, gone on submitting to what I was silly enough to call my "destiny." . . . I would have gone away without a word; and, credulous, innocent easy dupe that I was, just to prove to you, my beloved big sister, that I had profited by your noble lessons, so splendidly disinterested, I would have made believe that I shared your joy . . . that I was calling a blessing on your happiness, built up out of mine that you had demolished! . . . But the god of chance was juster and took pity

The Cloud That Lifted

on me, and opened my eyes! . . . And now it is chance that guides my steps, chance is my master and since it has come, let it be welcome! . . . Its will is clear, since that will alone is just. . . . Chance has given me weapons, and weapons such that if I discarded them, I should be committing a crime! . . . I have nothing to do henceforth but to let chance act, to let myself go along the road in which chance leads me! . . . My hate and my conscience follow the same path, and to fulfil my duty now I have only just to destroy you, and it is done!

SONIA
You appal me! . . .

TATIANA
Ah! it stupefies you that any one should wake up like this! Shut eyes are not al-

The Cloud That Lifted

ways asleep! . . . Yes! yes! I appal you, and will appal you still more when you see that I do not pause or stay, that I go on to the very end, that I have other passions and another way of hate and another way of love than your passions of ice and your wax-doll loving! . . . I am not sprung from a race that measures and weighs this and that! . . . And I will show you what one does when one loves like a real being and not like a prudent chop-logic ghost; and the force of the hate will teach you to measure the strength of the love you never saw. . . .

Sonia

I see that you will sacrifice me, and I offer myself up to your hate. . . . But Axel! . . . Have you no consideration for him? . . . Do you hate him, too, then? . . .

The Cloud That Lifted

TATIANA

But he is the one I hate, since he is the one I love! . . . Do you really imagine, Sonia, that I would take the trouble to avenge myself on you! Do you know nothing at all of all the things that lie within love—what love is? . . . Why, if he did not love you, you wouldn't even exist! . . . Since you took him from me, since I have lost him, and since he is blind and could not distinguish the humble but unquenchable love that burned in secret from the great painted flames with which you dazzled his eyes . . . well, then! so much the worse for him! . . . I would rather, a thousand times rather, see him dead at my feet than alive in your arms. . . . There is nothing to be done; I simply leave everything to fate, fate that is merely justice coming from all sides! . . .

The Cloud That Lifted

No one will ever be able to say I did not do right! . . . for giving up the guilty means saving the innocent. . . . No one will ever be able to say that I harmed you when I prevented you from loving the man who killed . . . perhaps at your bidding . . . perhaps to gain a little time . . . or who knows what. . . .

SONIA

Tatiana!

TATIANA

How can I tell? . . . Can any one tell? . . . In all this affair, your heart, your words, your inmost thoughts are all filled with such a heap of lies, of treacherous tendernesses, of insulting kindnesses and counterfeit virtues, that one is bogged to the very neck the moment one ventures in it—

The Cloud That Lifted

[*A knock is heard on the door to to the left. Enter a servant who gives a note to* SONIA *who reads the address and says.*]

SONIA

It is a note from Tormassov addressed to both of us.

TATIANA

Good, open it and read it. . . .

SONIA

[*Reads.*] "Let whichever of you two inseparables receives this note call her friend at once. . . . It concerns a great piece of good news, one that is of interest to both of you and demands the presence of both!

"It is almost certain that we have got the murderer this time. He is a young

The Cloud That Lifted

man from Abo; he declares his name is Axel Thorild. If this is not an assumed name, which we shall very soon ascertain, it figures already in the reports of the secret police. It belongs to a most dangerous patriot, one of the hidden heads of the Scandinavian faction, who for some time past has been under special surveillance. Naturally he denies any share in the crime; but, besides the fact that he has often been seen prowling around your garden, the witness of whom I have told you already, without being absolutely definite, would possibly have less hesitation in recognizing him if he were not under suspicion himself. However this may be, the thing at the moment is to bring the culprit face to face with our good little Tatiana, so that she may decide finally and authoritatively. So as not

The Cloud That Lifted

to disturb you disagreeably, and also in order to hasten matters, and to confront him with her on the actual scene of the crime, I will bring him to you under proper guard. . . . You need have no fears! . . . at ten o'clock precisely. So let both of you be at the post of duty!"

Tatiana!

TATIANA

Well, then? . . . It's half-past nine now; there is n't a long time to wait; I'll go and change my dress. . . .

SONIA

Tatiana! . . . I implore you! . . . Tatiana! . . . I am yours. . . . I surrender; I bow down before you; I understand; I absolve you of blame! . . . I have been selfish, blind, unjust, as we are all too often when we are in love! I never knew

The Cloud That Lifted

you still loved him . . . that you loved him like this! . . . What would you have me do to win you to take pity? . . . Ah, never envy me again at all. . . . You are the victor! . . . If I have been overproud, if love gave me more happiness than I deserved, it is all crushed, and it is all over and ended! . . . Tatiana! . . . I hope even now that this is your vengeance, that it will stop at this and that you will be satisfied now. . . . You have everything in the hollow of your hand; we are at your mercy. . . . Does a generous soul demand more than this? For me, if you punish me, it is well. . . . It is just, indeed, since you think it just and because I never saw that you were suffering side by side with my blind love. . . . But he? . . . you forgot too completely that you still love him. . . .

The Cloud That Lifted

When we hate the thing we love, you see, it is all in vain; we love more deeply than we hate. . . . He went on his way, never knowing that he was hurting you. . . . You never told him you loved him like this. . . . He could not grieve or betray the thing he never knew. . . .

TATIANA

So you want me to tell a lie, then, to indicate some one else? . . . But would you do that if you were in my place? . . . You are too ready to forget that he killed your father . . . and killed him in circumstances that would look very suspious to anybody except a woman who is gaining a lover by it.

SONIA

Tatiana! you know how to strike where it hurts. . . . Tatiana, you can see it for

The Cloud That Lifted

yourself. I am at the end of my strength, and I don't know which evil to choose. . . . If our happiness vexed you—and I can almost understand that, since you loathe me—you see that now this happiness is not worth a tear from you, and that it is sad enough to break down all hate. . . . How am I to go on loving him? . . . How is he to love me? . . . Our love is lost, ruined . . . chance has willed it so . . . there is nothing more to be done. . . . But Axel's life is still in your hands. . . . He is the one we love; let us think only of him. . . . I am ready for anything. . . . Tatiana, listen to me. Tatiana, I will tell you. . . . I give up all idea of happiness. . . . I surrender my own share to win mercy for him. . . . Take it; I will go away, and I will disappear for ever. . . . Take it; he will come and will never know.

The Cloud That Lifted

TATIANA

Good, this second bargain offer is just what I was expecting, too. . . . How low will you stoop? . . . You amuse me and disgust me all at once. . . . So you have just offered me the goodly leavings of a happiness that is slipping away from you! . . . You imagine I am very simple and guileless in spite of what I have done. . . . When Axel is there, and Tormassov has asked me, "Is this the guilty man?" and when I've said "No," what will there be left for me? . . . You perceive, my good friend, I have not the slightest confidence. . . . And I can see you already, going away, the two of you together, free, happy, smiling, steeped in a happiness more and more intoxicating the more tragic it is. . . . You will both thank me as you pass by, in low tones, so that nobody can suspect anything. . . . And I, I will be left there, with empty hands, all desolate, alone, disarmed, impotent, baffled, sublime, but a stupid fool! . . .

Sonia
[*Rising from her seat.*] I can neither implore nor offer any more. . . . The hour is coming nearer. . . . So it is settled that when Axel is here you will accuse him? . . .

Tatiana
It is settled that I shall speak the truth. . . .

Sonia
Your truth. . . .

Tatiana
Nothing but the truth. . . .

The Cloud That Lifted

SONIA

Be it so; we will argue no more. . . . Do your worst. . . . Give him up, coldly, basely! . . . But look at me well, for when two living beings look at one another like this, there is something that vouches for their final true intentions far better than their speech, far better than their oaths can do. . . . Look at me, I tell you! . . . The very moment you ruin him— I do not need to finish. . . . I am sure that you see what my soul has in mind, what my whole being is thinking, everything that causes it to live, everything that can kill it. . . .

TATIANA

And do you in your turn look at me, and do not repeat your threat.

> [SONIA *is silent.* TATIANA *goes out, keeping her eyes fixed on her.*

The Cloud That Lifted

Presently there is a ring at the outer door of the house. SONIA *goes to a secretaire standing in a corner of the room, takes a small revolver from it and puts it down, within reach of her hand, on the table near which she proceeds to sit down. Enter* TORMASSOV.]

Scene II

[Sonia; Tormassov.]

Tormassov

[*Hardly able to control himself for joy.*] Good evening, Sonia! . . . You are feeling better than you did yesterday? . . . You are looking perfectly splendid. . . . Did you have my little note? . . .

Sonia

Yes. . . . And what then? . . .

Tormassov

Are you pleased? . . . Are you glad? . . .

Sonia

Yes . . . although . . .

The Cloud That Lifted

TORMASSOV

Although what? . . .

SONIA

We can't be sure yet. . . .

TORMASSOV

We know already . . . we know already . . . and then we *shall* know . . . we shall know. . . . You will see. . . . Where is Tatiana? . . .

SONIA

She is coming. . . .

TORMASSOV

She does n't know, then? . . .

SONIA

Yes, yes, she has gone to change her dress, I think.

The Cloud That Lifted

TORMASSOV

That's just a woman all over! . . . On the day of judgment they will be late all for that "other frock." . . . Fortunately there are good theologians who maintain that they are not to have any dresses at all, *"du tout point,"* as my pet poet Malherbe puts it. Well now, and what do you say about it all?

SONIA

About what? . . .

TORMASSOV

About my capture, of course! . . . You don't look as though you believed it, or appreciated it. . . . And I fancied you would jump for joy, acclaim me, kiss me! . . . No, but this time I think I have been prompt and lucky with my task. . . . Ah, I've lost no time! . . . For

The Cloud That Lifted

the last two days now I have been grouping together certain facts that were not lacking in significance, and now it is all daylight, everything dovetails together, and it all corroborates itself. . . . The witness who ran into him . . . the police reports on the other plots, his political attitude, his habits, and the secret budget about him. . . . In short, there's nothing wanting now but Tatiana's evidence, which will be final and decisive. . . . Everything depends on that. . . . Meanwhile I would n't give much for his life, hanging on a yes or a no. . . . But what are you thinking of? . . . You don't seem to be taking any very great interest in what I am saying? . . .

SONIA

Where is he? . . .

The Cloud That Lifted

TORMASSOV

In the antechamber, between two stout guards. . . . He is young and elegant and distinguished-looking.

SONIA

I want to see him before Tatiana. . . . Bring him in.

TORMASSOV

That's easy. . . .

SONIA

But free. . . . He must be at liberty. . . . I don't want the guards. . . .

TORMASSOV

I understand. . . . It hasn't come to prison yet. . . . Nor what is to follow. . . . In any case, he is a gentleman and won't make a scene. . . . He seems to be

The Cloud That Lifted

resigned, and he does n't struggle. . . . They are all the same. . . . Great heroes before. . . . The world is all too narrow to hold their mighty spirit. . . . But once they are caught, good-bye! . . . They collapse like puppets when you cut the strings. . . . And then of course we won't lose sight of him. . . . I 'll bring him in. . . .

> [TORMASSOV *goes out by the door on the left and comes back next moment bringing* AXEL *into the drawing-room.*]

Scene III

[Sonia; Tormassov; Axel.]

Tormassov

[*To* Axel.] Over here, if you please; will you be good enough to come nearer the light? . . . [*To* Sonia.]. Do you recognize him? . . .

Sonia

[*Who has exchanged a swift look of misery with* Axel.] No!

Tormassov

You don't recollect. . . . You've never seen him? . . .

The Cloud That Lifted

Sonia

Never. . . .

Tormassov

And you, monsieur, what are your feelings face to face with your victim's daughter? . . . I am not going to make any phrases about it, but it is a grave and decisive moment. . . . It is still within your power in some degree to lessen your guilt. . . . If you will make a confession spontaneously and of your own accord, I guarantee that it will be counted in your favour. In a moment, when the witness on whom your fate depends has recognized you, it will be too late. . . . What is the use of standing out against the evidence.

Axel

What evidence do you see, monsieur?

The Cloud That Lifted

. . . I can only repeat what I have told you already. . . . "If this witness identifies me, that witness must either be deceived or be deceiving you."

TORMASSOV

She can't possibly be deceived; she saw you as clearly as I see you at this moment, and has declared she could recognize the murderer in a crowd. . . . As for deceiving us, why should she do that? . . . Mademoiselle Tatiana is the best and truest friend of Mademoiselle de Bielensky, and Mademoiselle de Bielensky will herself declare to you that her friend's evidence is as certain and trustworthy as that of her own eyes. . . . Is it not so, Sonia? . . . [*Sonia does not reply.*] Sonia! . . .

SONIA

What is it? . . .

The Cloud That Lifted

Tormassov

You are not listening to me. . . . Well, then, I am not sorry that there is an opportunity, before Mademoiselle Tatiana arrives, of making this gentleman understand the value, the infallible nature, of this evidence. Isn't that so, Sonia? . . . Tell monsieur what you think of it. . . .

Sonia

I think I hear her in the garden. . . . Yes, she is singing. . . . She does not know it is after ten and that we are waiting for her here.

Tatiana

[*Outside, singing as she passes in front of the windows at the back.*]

> L'amant dit à la belle:
> Où est la vérité?

The Cloud That Lifted

La vérité, dit-elle,
 Qui donc s'en fut douté,
La vérité, dit-elle,
 Est morte et enterrée.

[*In the silence that has fallen after the song, she is heard murmuring, as she tries to open the glass door at the back:* Heavens! how stiff this key is, how hard this door is to open. . . . Ah, at last. . . . It's giving. . . ." *She comes in immediately, pretending not to see* AXEL *or* TORMASSOV, *and, turning her back to them, she goes straight to the table near which* SONIA *is standing.*]

Scene IV

[Sonia; Tatiana; Axel; Tormassov.]

Tatiana

[*To* Sonia.] What time is it, Sonia? . . . Oh, the lovely moonlight on the lilacs all in bloom! . . . Look, you can see it from here. . . . [*Catching sight of the little revolver on the table.*] Ah, you have found the little revolver I gave you the day I arrived! . . . Where was it? . . . I thought it was lost. . . . What a funny little thing it is! . . . Do you think it could make a real wound? . . . Is it loaded? . . . Why, there's a spot of rust! . . . I'll take it to my room.

The Cloud That Lifted

. . . What? . . . You don't answer? . . . What is the matter? . . .

TORMASSOV

[*Coming up to* TATIANA *and laying his hand on her shoulder.*] Tatiana!

TATIANA

Oh! . . . it's you, is it? . . . I hadn't noticed you were there. . . . It's ten already. . . . I didn't imagine it was. . . . And your prisoner, when are we to see him? . . . Have you brought him? . . . Where is he? . . .

TORMASSOV

Here he is; look at him. . . .

TATIANA

Where is he? . . . Who? . . . This gentleman? . . .

The Cloud That Lifted

TORMASSOV

Yes, look closely at him; this is the man. . . .

TATIANA

He? . . . No, I don't know him. . . . I have never seen him before. . . .

TORMASSOV

Are you sure? . . .

TATIANA

Indeed, yes. . . . This gentleman is much taller . . . much handsomer. . . . So what are you going to do with him?

TORMASSOV

Nothing. [*To* AXEL.] Monsieur, you are at liberty, for the present, but I advise you to be more circumspect in your conduct in future.

The Cloud That Lifted

TATIANA

Do you know what I have just been seeing? . . . The beauty of the night, and that was enough for me. . . . [*Looking at* AXEL *and bursting into laughter.*] Heavens! how embarrassed he looks!

> [*She goes out and is heard still chuckling and laughing as she gets further away. After she has gone there is silence, and then, just as* TORMASSOV *moves towards the antechamber saying,* "I must tell the guards," *a shot is heard in the adjoining room.*]

TORMASSOV

What is that?

SONIA

Tatiana!

The Cloud That Lifted

AXEL

[*Forgetting himself.*] Go to her!
 [SONIA *dashes into the next room and is heard calling out,* "Tatiana! Tatiana! What have you done?" *Then she reappears on the threshold, holding up* TATIANA, *who is fainting.*]

SONIA

Help me! . . . She is falling . . . She is dying!
 [AXEL *and* TORMASSOV *hurry to her and carry* TATIANA *to the divan.*]

TATIANA

[*In the death-rattle. Pointing to her heart.*]
It's here! . . . it's all over. Where is Tormassov? . . .

The Cloud That Lifted

TORMASSOV

Here. . . . Don't speak.

TATIANA

Yes, it was I . . . you are not to search further.

TORMASSOV

What is she saying? . . .

SONIA

She is delirious. . . .

TATIANA

No . . . it was I . . . you know . . . Enough.

[*She falls back on the divan.*]

CURTAIN

www.ingramcontent.com/pod-product-compliance
Lightning Source LLC
LaVergne TN
LVHW031629070426
835507LV00024B/3405